NATIONAL GEOGRAPHIC KIDS

HUMAN FOOTPRINT

EVERYTHING YOU WILL EAT, USE, WEAR, BUY, AND THROW OUT IN YOUR LIFETIME

BY ELLEN KIRK

NATIONAL GEOGRAPHIC

WASHINGTON, D.C.

Contents

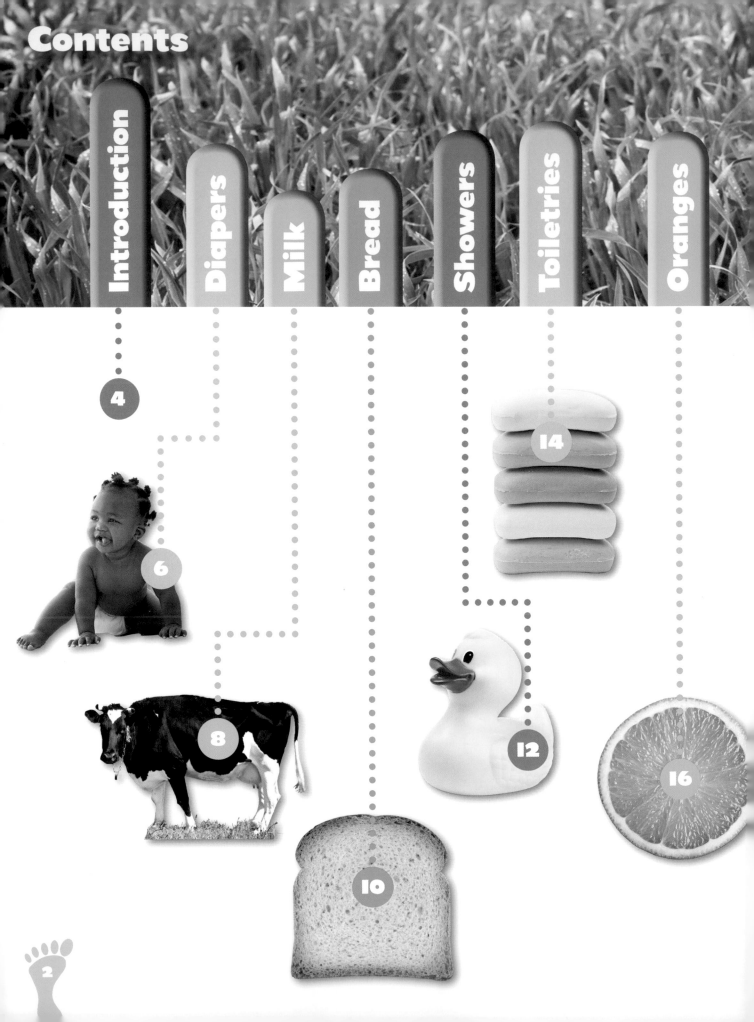

2

Your **human footprint** is the mark you make on the Earth.

You're only one person in a country (the United States) that has 308,000,000 (that's 308 million) people on a planet (Earth) that has 6,800,000,000 (that's 6 billion, 8 hundred million) people.

So, with all those people could your small human footprint really make a difference? Yes. You matter. What you do adds up.

In your lifetime you'll munch through 12 shopping carts full of candy bars. (Yum!) You'll drive 627,000 miles in a car. And that's just a tiny toe of your human footprint.

In this book you'll see pictures and read numbers describing what you'll eat, drink, use, and throw away in your lifetime. "You" really means the average American—a person who lives 77.75 years.

The pictures have been set up—not doctored—to show the numbers exactly. The number of soda cans in the picture on page 20 matches the number of sodas our average American will drink in a lifetime—43,371.

Read on and discover how amazingly BIG your human footprint really is—and how you can make it smaller while still having plenty of fun.

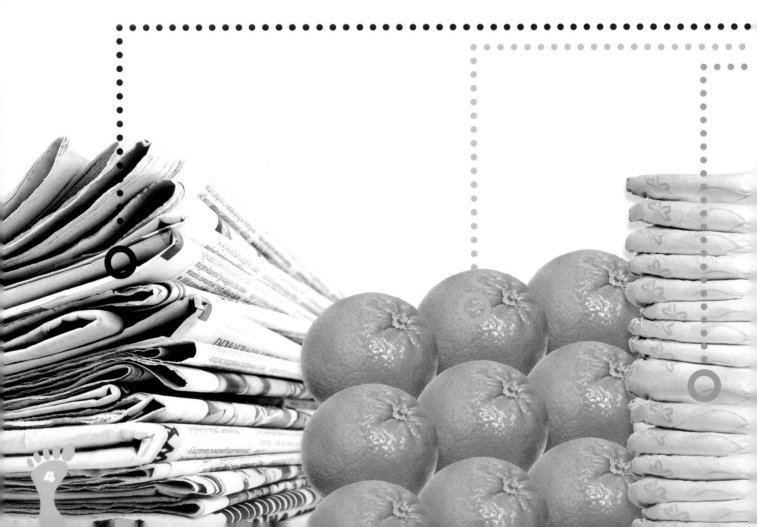

Here's your score...

5,054 Newspapers in your lifetime

12,888 Oranges in your lifetime

3,796 Diapers in your lifetime

12,129 Hamburger Buns in your lifetime

31,350 Gallons of Gas in your lifetime

It takes a **1/2** pint of crude oil to make the plastic lining of just **1** disposable diaper. That adds up to **1,898** pints for each baby!

Moms, dads and babysitters toss out **18 billion** disposable diapers each year in the United States. That's enough to make a diaper trail around the Earth **90** times.

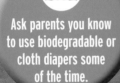

Ask parents you know to use biodegradable or cloth diapers some of the time.

Ooooh, Baby!
The first disposable diaper was made in 1949—out of a shower curtain and absorbent paper.

It could take **500** years for the disposable diapers we use today to biodegrade.

You'll drink **13,056** pints of milk in your lifetime.

It takes **12 pounds of milk** to make **1 gallon of ice cream!**

Look for ways to reuse your milk carton. Turn it into a planter!

Cows are cute, but they pollute! When a cow burps or farts, it releases methane, a gas that contributes to global warming. Each day, every cow on Earth pumps out around 40 gallons of methane. That about equals the pollution an SUV gives off on a 30-mile drive.

The average American consumes about **3** pints a week, **14** pints a month, **168** pints a year.

9,200,000 cows on **65,000** dairy farms work hard to produce the milk you consume. Every day, each cow eats **100** pounds of grass and other food and drinks **25** to **50** gallons of water.

It takes a lot of space to grow all that grass for all those cows: more than **20,000,000** acres. It's as if the entire state of Louisiana were reserved just for cows.

Every 3 years, you eat your weight in bread.

All the bread you'll eat makes **4,376** loaves. If you piled those loaves onto a scale, they would weigh just over **2** tons—close to what a full-grown hippopotamus weighs.

If you put all the wheat fields in America side by side, they would equal an area the size of the state of Wyoming.

All of those sandwiches and pieces of toast will add up to

87,520

slices of bread.

Reuse the plastic bag your bread comes in. Wrap your lunch sandwich in it.

Pizza crust is made from wheat, too. Americans eat **350** slices of pizza a second.

This parade of 28,433 rubber ducks shows all the showers you'll take in your lifetime.

12

To wash your hands, water the lawn, and flush the toilet, you'll send another **1.2 million** gallons spinning down the drain. With that much water, you could fill **4** Olympic-size swimming pools.

That's just ducky:
Because kids and adults are working hard to use less water, the amount consumed in the United States has plunged by 25 percent since the 1970s (even though the population has gone way up!).

Is there a leaky faucet in your house? Ask your parents to fix it. If you stop a faucet from leaking 1 drop each second, you'll save 2,700 gallons of water in a year.

To stay clean in a lifetime, you will use 656 bars of soap, 198 bottles of shampoo, 389 tubes of toothpaste, 272 containers of deodorant, and 156 toothbrushes!

Your hair grows about 1/2 inch per month. That doesn't sound like much, but it adds up. By the time you're 12, your hair will have grown 6 feet. No wonder you need so much shampoo!

14

The average American uses **10** different body products every day. That includes lotion, makeup, and perfume—as well as soap and shampoo.

To create all those gels, creams, and sweet-smelling liquids, companies use more than **5,000** different ingredients. When we rinse our faces and bodies at the end of the day, we wind up washing most of those chemicals down the drain. There, they mix together in combinations that nobody planned. That's wilder than any science-fair project!

Record for the world's longest hair: 18 feet, 5.54 inches!

To get from the grove to the store where you'll buy them, those oranges will travel a total of **23** million miles. That's the same as traveling to the moon and back **50** times.

9 out of **10** oranges grown in Florida are not eaten. They're squeezed—for orange juice.

12,888

is the number of oranges you will eat.

Instead of buying orange juice in a carton or bottle, squeeze your own!

A single orange tree can bear fruit for more than **100** years.

An **orange** is really a kind of **berry.**

The sugar from all those candy bars totals **1,055** pounds. That is the same as **211 5-pound** bags of sugar!

Make candy wrapper jewelry! Since wrappers are made out of different plastics, it isn't easy to recycle them.

child's **playtime** candy

5 1/3 lbs Value Bag

The first American chocolate bar was made in **1894**. But they didn't get really popular until World War I, when they became soldiers' favorite snacks.

American candy makers use more than **320** million pounds of peanuts, **759** million pounds of cocoa beans, **2.3** billion pounds of sugar, and **1.04** billion pounds of milk each year.

You will eat **14,518** candy bars, which is enough to fill **12** shopping carts!

In your lifetime, you will drink an astounding 43,371

Each day, **178** million cans of soda are popped open across the country. That's more than **2,000** cans per second.

The sugar in 1 can of soda equals 10 sugar cubes.

If you lined up all those cans, they'd stretch **3.42** miles. That's **50** football fields—with end zones!

cans of soda.

Every year, you'll buy **48** new things to wear.

To make room in your closet for those new outfits, you'll toss out **68** pounds of T-shirts, jeans, and other old clothes. Every year!

- a little cotton
- 1/3 pound of chemicals
- 528 gallons of water

It took all that to make this shirt.

You will spend **$52,972** on your clothes in your lifetime.

Be proud to wear hand-me-downs—they're recycled clothes!

If you weighed all your dirty laundry for a year, it would tip the scales at **500** pounds.

Every year, Americans throw out **4.6 million** tons of tires. Some old tires are ground up and made into turf for sports fields and soft padding for playgrounds.

You will drive the equivalent of **25 times** around the world.

The parts of the cars you'll own will travel farther than your complete cars will ever drive. In some cars, the seatbelts come from Sweden, the doors from Thailand, and the stereo and electric wiring from China.

You will own 12 cars in your lifetime.

Help your parents save gas: Don't carry junk in your trunk! For every 100 pounds of extra stuff in your car, your gas mileage can drop by 2 percent.

You and your fellow Americans throw away **694** plastic bottles a second.

Wear me! Many fleece jackets contain threads made from recycled plastic bottles.

4 billion pounds of plastics are recycled each year in the **United States**, saving enough energy (oil and natural gas) to heat **2.1 million** homes.

Over a lifetime, each of us will also toss out **29,700** pounds of plastic packaging—plastic food wrap, plastic grocery bags, plastic garbage bags, plastic toy boxes, and more!

Almost all plastic is made from oil or natural gas.

No one knows how long plastic takes to break down. Once it's in a landfill, it may stay there forever.

When you're out and about, don't throw it out! Take your soda and water bottles back home to recycle.

Your human footprint

12 cars

7 washing machines

5 refrigerators

15 computers

3,796 disposable diapers

$52,972 worth of clothes

5,054 newspapers

4,376 loaves of bread

How to Shrink Your Human Footprint: 7 Important Tips

1. Use less plastic. Bring a cloth bag when you shop, and use refillable water bottles.

2. Ask your parents to use ENERGY STAR® approved light bulbs. If every American home replaced a standard bulb with an energy-efficient one, we would save enough energy to light 3 million homes for a year.

3. Eat more vegetables! It takes only 6 gallons of water to grow a serving of lettuce. Compare that to the 2,600 gallons it takes to produce a serving of steak.

Now you know just how BIG your footprint is. Next step: Try to make it smaller. The world will thank you!

9,917 pounds of potatoes

43,371 cans of soda

13,056 pints of milk

12 shopping carts full of candy bars

28,433 rubber ducks, representing 28,433 showers

Recycle your cans. takes 95 percent ss energy to make aluminum can from cycled aluminum than om new materials.

5. Walk or ride a bike. Your family saves gas by leaving the car behind.

6. Recycle your batteries and use rechargeable batteries when you can. When batteries end up in landfills, toxic chemicals seep into the ground, harming the environment.

7. Don't waste food. Enough edible food to feed 49 million people ends up in landfills in the United States each year.

LET'S DO SOMETHING GOOD FOR THE PLANET

USE ONLY WHAT YOU NEED, AND HAVE FUN DOING IT!

Collect rainwater, then use it to water your plants and wash your car.

Turn down the heat in your home—just 2 degrees can save lots of energy.

Unplug TVs, microwaves, and other appliances you don't use much. It can cut your electricity use by 10 percent!

National Geographic's *Human Footprint* TV show is the main source of facts in this book. Additional sources are:

pp. 4-5: Introduction
• U.S. population updated constantly on the Census Bureau website. See the population clock in the right-hand corner. http://www.census.gov/

pp. 6-7: Diapers
• Invention of disposable diapers: Facts On File, Inc., 2002. *American Women's History Online*, "Donovan, Marion." http://www.fofweb.com

pp. 8-9: Milk
• Amount of milk in ice cream: Umpqua Dairy, Roseburg, Oregon. http://www.umpquadairy.com/page/cool-cow-facts
• Methane from cows: "How to Stop Cows Burping is the New Fieldwork on Climate Change," *The Times*, July 10, 2007. http://www.timesonline.co.uk/tol/news/science/article2051364.ece
• From cow to grocery store: New England Dairy Council. http://www.newenglanddairycouncil.org

pp. 10-11: Bread
• Weight of a hippopotamus: Grolier Online, *Amazing Animals of the World, 2009*, "Hippopotamus." http://ama.grolier.com

pp. 12-13: Showers
• Leaky faucet water waste: *National Geographic Green Tips for Kids*. http://kids.nationalgeographic.com/Stories/SpaceScience/Green-tips
• Decline in water use: "Americans Use Less Water," *USA Today*, March 11, 2009. http://www.usatoday.com/news/2004-03-11-water-usat_x.htm

pp. 14-15: Toiletries
• Americans use 10 body products per day: Saving Face: "How Safe Are Cosmetics and Body Care Products?" *Scientific American*, May 5, 2009. http://www.scientificamerican.com/article.cfm?id=how-safe-are-cosmetics
• Rate of hair growth: Grolier Online, *The New Book of Knowledge, 2009*, "Hair and Hairstyling." http://nbk.grolier.com

pp. 16-17: Oranges
• Oranges bear fruit for 100 years: Grolier Online, *The New Book of Knowledge, 2009*, "Oranges and Grapefruit." http://nbk.grolier.com/
• Nine out of 10 oranges used for juice: Centers for Disease Control, Fruit & Vegetable of the Month. http://www.fruitsandveggiesmatter.gov/month/orange.html
• An orange is a type of berry: Grolier Online, *Encyclopedia Americana, 2009*, "Orange (fruit)." http://ea.grolier.com

pp. 18-19: Candy Bars
• First American chocolate bar: National Confectioners Association, "Candy Bars." http://www.candyusa.com
• Ingredients in candy: National Confectioners Association, "Profile of the U.S. Candy Industry (2007 data)." http://www.candyusa.com

pp. 20-21: Soda Cans
• Sugar cubes in soda: "20 Things You Didn't Know About Sugar," *Discover*, October, 2009.

pp. 24-25: Car Parts
• 4.5 million tons of tires: Rubber Manufacturers Association, "More Old Tires Put to Good Uses," Press Release, 2009. http://rma.org/newsroom/
• Junk in your trunk: U.S. Environmental Protection Agency, "Driving More Efficiently." http://www.fueleconomy.gov/feg/driveHabits.shtml

pp. 26-27: Plastic Bottles
• Most plastic is made from oil or natural gas and will never break down: Grolier Online, *The New Book of Knowledge, 2009*, "Plastics." http://nbk.grolier.com
• Fleece made from plastic: "Gear Test with Tricia Chism, Fitness Instructor: Running in Your Recyclables," *The New York Times*," November 27, 2008. http://nytimes.com
• Four billion pounds of plastics recycled: American Chemistry Council, "Fact Sheet: Plastics Recycling in the United States" (2006 data). http://www.americanchemistry.com/s_plastics/sec_con.asp?CID=1102&DID=8811

pp 28-29: Your Human Footprint
• Tip 7: *National Geographic Green Tips for Kids*. http://kids.nationalgeographic.com/Stories/SpaceScience/Green-ti

pp. 30-31: Your Human Footprint
• Unplug TVs: Lawrence Berkeley National Laboratory, "Standby Power: Frequently Asked Questions." http://standby.lbl.gov/faq.html

This book was created by jacob packaged goods LLC (jpgglobal.com)

Written by: Denise Rinaldo, Ragan O'Malley, and Ellen Kirk

Design: LuAnn Graffeo-Blonkowski, Ellen Jacob

National Geographic Children's Books: Jennifer Emmett, Jonathan Halling, Lori Epstein, Grace Hill

All photos copyright © Roy Gumpel/ Touch Productions Ltd. unless otherwise noted below.

Cover background, 1, 2-3, 4-5, all inset images, 30-31, photo composite, 32 copyright © Shutterstock.

The book is based on the Preserve Our Planet National Geographic Channel presentation, *Human Footprint*.

For more information, check out *Human Footprint* on DVD or go to the website http://channel.nationalgeographic.com/channel/human-footprint/

Founded in 1888, the National Geographic Society is one of the largest nonprofit scientific and educational organizations in the world. It reaches more than 285 million people worldwide each month through its official journal, NATIONAL GEOGRAPHIC, and its four other magazines; the National Geographic Channel; television documentaries; radio programs; films; books; videos and DVDs; maps; and interactive media. National Geographic has funded more than 8,000 scientific research projects and supports an education program combating geographic illiteracy.

For more information, please call 1-800-NGS LINE (647-5463) or write to the following address:
National Geographic Society
1145 17th Street N.W., Washington, D.C. 20036-4688 U.S.A.

Visit us online at www.nationalgeographic.com/books

For librarians and teachers: www.ngchildrensbooks.org

More for kids from National Geographic: kids.nationalgeographic.com

For information about special discounts for bulk purchases, please contact National Geographic Books Special Sales: ngspecsales@ngs.org

For rights or permissions inquiries, please contact National Geographic Books Subsidiary Rights: ngbookrights@ngs.org

Library of Congress Cataloging-in-Publication Data available upon request

Trade edition ISBN: 978-1-4263-0767-6

Printed in U.S.A.

11/WOR/2